THE STORY OF
HANDEL'S MESSIAH
1741-1784

The Story of Handel's *Messiah*

1741-1784

A SHORT POPULAR HISTORY BY

WATKINS SHAW

With eight illustrations and fourteen music examples

NOVELLO & COMPANY LTD
160 Wardour Street London W1

FIRST PRINTED IN JULY 1963

© Novello and Company Limited 1963

Set in Monotype Garamond
Printed and bound in England
by Novello and Company Limited
London W.1

CONTENTS

PREFACE

ALTHOUGH this little book is intended for general reading and interest and has no scholarly purpose, it is nevertheless based on the intensive investigation undertaken for my larger and fully-documented work, *A Textual and Historical Companion to Handel's Messiah* (Novello, in the press).

It is not, however, simply a diluted version of the *Textual Companion*, but contains other material not appropriate to that book. A certain amount of this is based on my own original work (particularly in Chapter VII), some of it already published in various journals and some of it hitherto unpublished.

The sources of my quotations are listed on p. 75. Those known to me only through Otto Erich Deutsch's *Handel: A Documentary Biography* (1955) are here reproduced by kind permission of the publishers, Messrs A. & C. Black, Ltd. I am grateful also to those who have so kindly permitted the reproduction of fac-similes and pictures as listed on p. 9.

Worcester
4 June 1962   Watkins Shaw

LIST OF PLATES

The kind permission of the present owners to reproduce certain plates is gratefully acknowledged as follows:

Plates I and VI: the Warden and Fellows of St. Michael's College, Tenbury Wells, Worcs.; Plate II: The Viscount Curzon; Plates IV and VII: Gerald Coke, Esq.; Plate V: The University of California, Berkeley 4, U.S.A.

Plate III is reproduced from the fac-simile published by Friedrich Chrysander (Hamburg, 1892).

Chapter I

The composition of Messiah

1741

HANDEL was fifty-six years old when he sat down in his London home on 22 August 1741 to start work on *Messiah*. He had in front of him a remarkable libretto, compiled from Holy Scripture by Charles Jennens. Jennens, a friend of the composer, was a Leicestershire squire whose seat was at Gopsal, commemorated by the name of one of Handel's hymn-tunes. From what we know of him, Jennens was a conceited figure of no special ability and was unlikely to have been the author of any work of artistic sensibility. Yet the fact remains that his selection of scriptural texts for the 'book' of *Messiah* amounts to little short of a work of genius. With the exception of a few verses from St Luke's Gospel dealing with the Nativity, Jennens avoided all narrative: his libretto is a meditation on the significance of our Lord as Messiah in Christian thought and belief. Although in 'He was despised' and 'All they that see him' we think of Christ's Passion, and in 'I know that my redeemer liveth' and 'The trumpet shall sound' of His Resurrection and victory over death, these events are not directly referred to. The kernel to Jennens's compilation is expressed in some words from the Epistles which he himself supplied to form a prefix to the word-book of the oratorio:

> And without Controversy, great is the Mystery of Godliness:
>> God was manifested in the Flesh, justified by the Spirit, seen of Angels, preached among the Gentiles, believed on in the World, received up in Glory.
>
> In whom are hid all the Treasures of Wisdom and Knowledge.
>> (1 Timothy iii, 16; Colossians ii, 3)

It is specially interesting to observe how widely Jennens ranged the Scriptures for his texts. Not only Gospels and Epistles, Psalms and Isaiah are drawn upon, but also little-known parts of the Bible such as Haggai ('Thus saith the Lord') and Zechariah ('And he shall purify'). Particularly remarkable is the way the texts are married together from widely separated sources. The words of 'I know that my redeemer liveth' are so familiar to us in the form devised by Jennens and set by Handel that we do not readily realize how they are drawn partly from the Book of Job, partly from the First Epistle to the Corinthians.

Such a libretto, entirely in scriptural words and wholly non-dramatic, is unusual in Handel's works. His genius was markedly dramatic. This is disclosed not only in his long series of works for the operatic stage, but in his many other compositions, like *Samson*, *Solomon*, and *Theodora*, written in the form of the dramatic oratorio which he shaped for himself. In this respect, therefore, *Messiah* is not typical of his oratorios, which makes it all the more remarkable that it has seized the public imagination to a degree unparalleled by any of his other works. One of the factors undoubtedly contributing to this is its religious appeal as a setting of an exalted theme in the noble language of the Authorized Version of the Bible. For his part in it, Charles Jennens must be given ungrudging credit.

On his original manuscript score Handel noted the dates as his work progressed. Starting on 22 August (a Saturday) he reached the end of Part One (a hundred pages) six days later, 28 August; by 6 September he had completed a further 107 pages to the end of 'Hallelujah'; and on Saturday, 12 September he finished the whole work in outline, having written a total of 259 pages. Then he went over it again filling out the instrumentation and finally added that the work was 'ausgefüllt' on 14 September. Altogether his work took twenty-four days. This was certainly quick, but it was not unusual with Handel, and it would be wrong to sentimentalize the circumstance by imagining that this speed was in some way attributable to a special factor of inspiration connected with the subject-matter of *Messiah*.

A certain amount of his material lay ready to hand. As recently as July 1741 he had written two duets to Italian words. It was on one of these that he drew for the choruses 'And he shall purify' and 'His yoke is easy', and the other was used in 'For unto us a child is born' and 'All we like sheep have gone astray'. One cannot fail to observe a lightness of texture and pre-ponderance of two-part writing which marks the origin of these choruses. At the same time, Handel's additions to his basic material are very striking—the impressive *adagio* ending to 'All we like sheep have gone astray', the sonorous four-part passage at the words 'that they may offer unto the Lord an offering in righteousness' in 'And he shall purify', and the choral ejaculations 'Wonderful, Counsellor, the mighty God, the ever-lasting Father, the Prince of Peace' in 'For unto us a child is born'.

Even Handel's amazing master-craftsmanship did not mean that everything was written down white-hot

Ex. 1

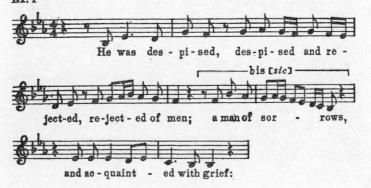

He was des-pi-sed, des-pi-sed and re-

bis [*sic*]

ject-ed, re-ject-ed of men; a man of sor - rows,

and ac-quaint - ed with grief:

without preliminary sketches. Two or three scraps of
notes for *Messiah* have, as it happens, survived. The
original form of 'He was despised' is very interesting,
and reveals the extent to which it was later improved.
(see p. 13). A further pair of jottings for 'Let us break
their bonds asunder' at first had the words 'Let all the
angels of God'. For 'Amen' there are no fewer than
seven experimental passages designed to test the over-
lapping imitation between the voices. The following
example is connected with the section now forming
bars 113-118 of the final chorus:

Ex. 2

Still more interesting than these rough notes are the
changes made in the score itself while Handel was
actually writing. One can tell from the position of the
alterations, and from how they are made, that in many
cases he had hardly begun some particular passage
when he immediately saw how it could be improved
before going any further. A very few examples must do
duty to indicate the wealth of similar fascinating
features.

In 'And the glory of the Lord' he first wrote as follows at bar 79:

Ex. 3

This phrase would surely have led directly to what is now bar 84. But before passing to bar 80, the composer turned the first note of the soprano part into a minim, crossed out the next two crotchets and inserted a rest, altered the alto and tenor parts to what we now have at bar 79, so continuing with the chorus in the form familiar to us.

In our next example, from 'Behold the Lamb of God', Handel proceeded somewhat further before changing his mind. After bar 26 he wrote the passage given below in small notes, but then crossed it out vigorously as soon as he had written it and continued with the present bar 27:

Ex. 4

The ending of 'And with his stripes we are healed' was at first designed as a perfect cadence:

Ex. 5

Handel deleted the passage printed here in small notes, moved his 'adagio' further back, doubled the values of the previous notes and placed a ⁀ sign over the C major chord, so producing the half-close we now know, leading directly into 'All we like sheep have gone astray'.

One last example: in the concluding bars of the whole work it may be seen how the compelling harmony before the pause was not the first thing to occur to the composer; nor was the eventual form of the first bar of the final *Adagio:*

Ex. 6

In this example the two bass notes marked (x) are conjectural. They were so heavily altered by Handel that neither the original nor the alteration is readable, and he resorted to writing the letter names of the notes as finally amended, thus: 'f' and 'd'.

PLATE I

George Frideric Handel
Oil-painting by or after Thomas Hudson

PLATE II

Charles Jennens
Oil-painting by Thomas Hudson, c. 1750

The wonder is that the manuscript is as clear as it is. As for errors and omissions, the number of these can only be described as minute for a work of such length. The small things liable to creep into any manuscript, even a fair copy made at leisure (which this certainly is not)—a missing dot, a missing accidental, an occasional error in pitch—these certainly occur, but not to any great extent in so long a work. In fact, if we had no contemporary fair copies, we should be able, without too much difficulty, to get nearly all we need from this manuscript. There are a few details which might give trouble, as they did to various early copyists. Such a one occurs in the instrumental bass to bars 63-4 of 'All we like sheep have gone astray' where, following Handel's change from *g, f, e, d* to *g, d, e, g*, the resulting double notes could be misleading:

Ex. 7

It is not only that such details are interesting, and sometimes important, in themselves. They also help us, in imagination, to look over the composer's shoulder as he is absorbed in the act of inventing, adapting, copying. It has been said that at one time it was still possible to see traces of the sand he sprinkled the pages of his manuscript with to dry the ink. Although I cannot vouch for that, it is a wonderful document to be privileged to examine. Its blots, its alterations, even its occasional failings, all vividly call up the scene and act of composition and Handel's impatience to get his thoughts down on paper. And it is an impressive testimony to the sureness and completeness of his immediate invention and craftsmanship as well as to the roughly efficient clarity of his rapid script.

An examination of the manuscript makes it obvious

that Handel carried out certain adjustments to it after he had written the final date at the end. The most extensive of these concerns the 'Pastoral Symphony'. As he first wrote it, this consisted of eleven bars only. Later he extended it by writing an additional ten bars on an extra slip of paper which is now bound into the volume. He altered the ending of his original piece to lead to the added section and then marked the first section to be repeated. This brought about the familiar *da capo* form of his movement. Nevertheless, Handel did not forget his original short form; as we shall see in due course, he revived this at a later date.

A fair copy of the completed manuscript was then written out by the composer's amanuensis, Johann Christoph Schmidt (anglicized as John Christopher Smith), his old friend from Ansbach who assisted him in England with the management of affairs. This consisted of two volumes which are now in the library of St Michael's College, Tenbury Wells, Worcestershire. The original autograph manuscript is now in the British Museum, having formed part of the Royal Library from about 1774 (temp. George III) until Queen Elizabeth II presented that Library to the British Museum in 1957.

So far from being exhausted by his task, Handel then proceeded to compose *Samson*, on which he worked from 29 September to 29 October; after which, with very little interval for rest, he set off for Dublin, where he arrived on 18 November, having been held up *en route* at Chester for some days.

Chapter II

Messiah *in its Original Form*

THE manuscript of which John Christopher Smith made a fair copy in the autumn of 1741 was very far from representing the last of Handel's work on the oratorio. As the years went by he re-wrote certain movements, and was wont also to revive earlier settings and to authorize transpositions for other voices. It is therefore not surprising that what we may call the 1741 version contains a good deal of music unfamiliar to listeners at the present time. It will be of interest to go through that form, noticing the settings which are not generally used today.

The first is 'But who may abide the day of his coming?' This was written for a bass soloist in 3-8 time and opens (as far as the first note of bar 16) in exactly the same way as the familiar setting. But it has only 136 bars, and there is no change of tempo and time-signature at the words 'For he is like a refiner's fire'. This short quotation indicates the style of the original setting at that point. By the side of the later version, this original form is tame and undistinguished.

Ex. 8

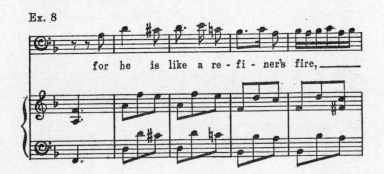

for he is like a re-fi-ner's fire,_____

'Rejoice greatly, O daughter of Zion' is the next movement whose first form is different from the familiar one. Here we find it in B flat for soprano, but in 12-8 time. In the example below the 12-8 form of bars 12-14 is given with the 4-4 version below for comparison, to show the relationship between them.

Ex. 9

The mere difference between the rhythmic patterns of
12-8 and 4-4 times is by no means all, however. This
12-8 version was very long—113 bars plus a *da capo*
repeat of the first 91¼ bars. As a point of interest, and
one of some importance later, it may be mentioned
that Handel observed the old convention of writing
the instrumental bass part of his 12-8 version in
common time, thus:

Ex. 10

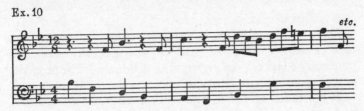

This procedure will be familiar to readers from such
things as certain movements in Corelli's sonatas and
also from Bach.

Proceeding further, we notice that 'He shall feed his
flock' is not divided between alto (F major) and
soprano (B flat, entering at 'Come unto him'); instead
the whole of it is in B flat for soprano, the music of the
first part being the same as that commonly sung by an
alto today, but written a fourth higher. The preceding
recitative, 'Then shall the eyes of the blind', is similarly
a fourth higher. It will not have escaped notice that in
his original form Handel wrote two long arias for
soprano—'Rejoice greatly' and 'He shall feed his
flock'—in succession, both in B flat, both in 12-8
time, albeit one of them *Allegro*, the other *Larghetto*.

In Part Two it should be mentioned first that the
original form of 'Thou art gone up on high' (for bass
soloist) is the one found in the various well-known
editions by Vincent Novello, W. T. Best, and Prout; in
the edition for which I am responsible this form is
placed in the Appendix.

On reaching 'Their sound is gone out' we find a big difference. Instead of the well-known chorus in E flat following the aria 'How beautiful are the feet' we find those words set for soprano soloist as the middle section of an aria whose opening is the familiar 'How beautiful are the feet' and whose conclusion is a repetition thereof. Thus we have:

How beautiful . . . Their sound is gone out . . .
How beautiful (repeated)

as a *dal segno* aria.

In Part Three there is no important difference, but 'The trumpet shall sound' is *da capo*, not, as now generally marked, *dal segno*, and 'O death, where is thy sting?' has 41 bars, not 24.

Such, then, so far as the movements are concerned, is *Messiah* 'as it was originally written'. It seems that Handel himself never performed it exactly so, and that it should be regarded as no more than a first draft. By this, one means only that all the original settings were never performed together on one occasion, not that every one of those discussed was never used. Yet it certainly seems probable that the *dal segno* form of 'How beautiful are the feet' was never performed by Handel, and this may well be true also of the bass form of 'But who may abide the day of his coming?'.

There is another aspect of the original manuscript to consider, and that is the instrumentation. This occupies from two staves (in many arias) to four staves (in most choruses and a number of arias), apart from the movements requiring trumpets and drums, which have extra staves for the purpose. Except for the trumpets and drums, Handel is unsystematic about labelling his staves. When he does so, it is to indicate violins and violas. His instrumental bass stave is never labelled. What instrumentation did he intend? In the arias there is no doubt he meant violins, with violas if there was a stave in the alto clef or if he marked the violin line 'e viola'. In the choruses, whether the composer actually marked them or not, it was the custom to use oboes. The task of drawing out the parts was very often left (as in this instance) to the common sense of copyists who would write parts based on the track of the violins or the chorus voices. If we do not use oboes in some such way we are not following Handel's practice, even though oboes are not mentioned in his manuscript. Similarly with the bass instrumental line: here not only cellos and double basses are required but also bassoons, reinforcing in the choruses throughout, and probably playing in the louder orchestral passages of the arias. Finally, an organ and a harpsichord, again not specified in the score but assumed by all composers of Handel's period, are needed to supply a rhythmic and harmonic background to the choruses (organ) and recitatives and arias (harpsichord). Composers did not write down such a part, and it must be furnished by a modern editor if not by the performer himself.

Why, it may be asked, did Handel not make all this explicit in his score? The answer is that the conventions governing it were so thoroughly understood that it was all taken for granted. In using oboes and bassoons in such a way, we are realizing, not altering, the composer's intentions, within the discretionary limits he left his copyists. 'Additional accompaniments'—from Mozart to Beecham—are quite another matter. The objection to these is that they rescore the work in the style of other periods, so altering Handel's intention. He was a sufficient master to score in the way he wanted in the style then current; and this we must maintain if we are to re-create the full effect of his characteristic expression.

Chapter III

The First Performances

HANDEL'S visit to Ireland in 1741-2 was the outcome of an invitation by the Duke of Devonshire, the Lord Lieutenant. This probably took the form of a suggestion that a series of subscription concerts in the new Music Room in Fishamble street would be well supported, and also a promise of vice-regal patronage. There is no doubt that Handel composed *Messiah* with this visit in mind. Whether, from the first, he intended that it should be performed for charity is uncertain, though it is quite probable. However these things may be, it is a fact that *Messiah* received its première in the year 1742 in the Irish capital.

With his Irish season in view, Handel arranged for a Mr Maclaine, an organist, and his wife, a soprano, to cross over to Dublin, as well as Signora Avolio, also a soprano. Of the Maclaines virtually nothing else is known; Avolio, however, sang also for Handel in London. Another singer, Mrs Cibber, may perhaps have gone to Ireland on her own account. Primarily an actress rather than a vocalist, she appeared at the Theatre Royal, Dublin in December 1741, in Steele's play *The Conscious Lovers*. The leading instrumentalist in Dublin was Matthew Dubourg, master of the vice-regal band and a musician of standing already known to Handel; it was he who led the orchestra for the season.

Early in December, Handel publicly announced his subscription series of six concerts. From the beginning things went well for him and his performances were crowded. In writing to Jennens on 29 December 1741 to acknowledge the scripture quotations forming the preface to the *Messiah* libretto, Handel said:

The Nobility did me the honour to make amongst themselves
a Subscription for 6 Nights, which did fill a Room of 600
Persons, so that I needed not sell one single ticket at the
Door . . . Sigra Avolio, which I brought with me from
London, pleases extraordinary . . . as for the Instruments
they are really excellent, Mr Dubourgh being at the Head
of them, and the Musick sounds delightfully in this charming
Room . . . I cannot sufficiently express the kind treatment I
receive here . . . They propose already to have some more
Performances, when the 6 Nights of the Subscription are
over . . .[1]

Meanwhile, neither in his first series of six concerts (23
December 1741 to 10 February 1742) nor in the second
series (announced on 6 February) was there any
mention of *Messiah*. But early in March a committee
was at work to arrange 'a Performance designed for
the benefit of the Hospital [*i.e.*, Mercer's Hospital], the
Infirmary, and the Prisoners of the Marshalseas' and
there is no doubt that this was to be *Messiah*. The
following public announcement appeared on 27 March
1742:

For Relief of the Prisoners in the several Gaols, and for the
Support of Mercer's Hospital in Stephen's street, and of the
Charitable Infirmary on the Inn's Quay, on Monday the 12th
of April, will be performed at the Musick Hall in Fishamble
street, *Mr. Handel's new Grand Oratorio, called the* MESSIAH, in
which the Gentlemen of the Choirs of both Cathedrals will
assist, with some Concertos on the Organ, by Mr. Handell.
Tickets to be had at the Musick Hall, and at Mr. Neal's in
Christ Church-yard, at half a Guinea each. N.B. No Person
will be admitted to the Rehearsal without a Rehearsal Ticket,
which will be given gratis with the Ticket for the Performance when payed for.[2]

The rehearsal was a great success and was attended
by 'a most Grand, Polite, and Crowded Audience'.
The oratorio itself (described in one newspaper as
'this elegant Entertainment') was adjudged, with
enthusiastic hyperbole, 'to be the finest Composition
of Musick that ever was heard'. At the request of

'several persons of Distinction' the performance was postponed from 12 to 13 April; and, in order that the charities might benefit to the full from the largest possible attendance, an announcement was made asking if ladies 'would be pleased to come without Hoops' and gentlemen without swords, with the object of increasing the space available. In the event, 700 people attended. As for Handel's noble generosity in thus devoting to charity the first performance of what was to become his most renowned masterpiece, one cannot do better than quote the words of *Faulkner's Dublin Journal* for 17 April 1742:

> It is but Justice to Mr. Handel that the World should know he generously gave the Money arising from this Grand Performance, to be equally shared by the Society for relieving Prisoners, the Charitable Infirmary, and Mercer's Hospital, for which they will ever gratefully remember his Name.[3]

Each charity received £127.

The performance was repeated 'At the Particular Desire of several of the Nobility and Gentry' on 3 June, again with a public rehearsal. In view of the season of the year and in order 'to keep the Room as cool as possible, a Pane of Glass will be removed from the top of each of the Windows'[4]. The announcement does not mention charity. Whereas in April Handel had had no part in the selling of tickets, it was possible to obtain them this time, as for his other concerts, from his lodging in Abbey street. It seems likely, therefore, that the second performance was not for charity. This marked Handel's last public appearance in Ireland. In August *Faulkner's Dublin Journal* recorded that 'the celebrated Mr. Handel, so famous for his excellent Compositions and fine Performance with which he entertained this Town in the most agreeable Manner, embarked for England'.[5]

Perhaps it should be mentioned here that Handel's

earliest biographer, Mainwaring (whose anonymous
'Memoirs of the Life of Handel' appeared in 1760),
knew nothing of these Dublin performances. He
asserted that *Messiah* was first performed in London
before Handel's departure for Ireland. But, bearing in
mind the date when *Messiah* was completed (14
September), the time when the composer was occupied
with *Samson* (29 September to 29 October) and his
arrival in Dublin on 18 November after delay at
Chester, it is impossible to believe that any performance
of the work could have been arranged before Handel
left London.

In spite of the admiration it immediately won, no-
body connected with these performances in Dublin
could have had the least idea of the astonishing esteem
Messiah would earn in years to come, nor have foreseen
what deep curiosity there would be, after 200 years, about
the circumstances of its production. For such reasons
we may consider ourselves amazingly fortunate in
what can be pieced together about that now far-off
première. A great deal of useful information comes
from contemporary Dublin newspapers. It was an
Irish barrister named George Finlayson who, in 1849,
first drew attention to the announcement of the performance for charity. Soon afterwards (1852) another
Irish barrister, Horatio Townsend, published 'An
Account of the Visit of Handel to Dublin' after
investigating all the relevant newspapers and other
records. It is from his careful book that the quotations
already made in this chapter have been taken.

By good luck a few copies survived of the word-
book published in connexion with these performances.
They provide certain additional, detailed information.
It is with surprise that we read how 'But who may
abide the day of his coming?', 'Thou art gone up on
high' and 'Thou shalt break them' were sung in recitative form—as *recitativo secco*, in fact. The second of these

no longer exists, but this setting of 'Thou shalt break
them' illustrates the style:

Ex. 11

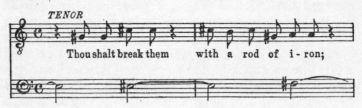

Another surprise awaits us after 'The Lord gave the
word'. Here, instead of any setting of 'How beautiful
are the feet . . . Their sound is gone out', we find
Handel has turned to a different part of the Bible and
written a movement, starting as a duet and then passing
into a chorus, to the following text from Isaiah:

> How beautiful are the feet of him that bringeth good tidings,
> tidings of salvation; that saith unto Zion, Thy God reigneth!
> Break forth into joy.

By a hundred-to-one chance it happens, out of the
mere handful of surviving copies of the word-book,
that the original owner of one of them jotted down the
singers' names against many of the solo movements.
We can well imagine him, with little elbow-room, in
the crowded auditorium, and forgive him for an occasional slip: he put 'Cibber' against 'Behold the Lamb
of God' when he surely intended it against 'He was
despised'. This copy of the word-book was found on a

Dublin book-stall by Professor Dowden, a Shakesperian scholar, who gave it to the organist of the Chapel Royal, Dublin, Dr J. C. Culwick; as a result, Culwick published a most interesting account of it in 1891 and afterwards presented the word-book to the British Museum.

In it we find Mrs. Cibber's name against 'Then shall the eyes of the blind'; this can only mean that she also sang 'He shall feed his flock'. As originally composed, this recitative and air was for soprano. It does so happen, however, in a few secondary manuscripts of *Messiah*, that they are both transposed down a fourth for alto, and we may therefore suppose that this alto form had its origin in the earliest performances. The same singer's name is mentioned against 'If God be for us'. Again, this must mean that a transposed form was used; and once more such a form (in C minor) survives in certain early manuscripts.

These two transpositions have some practical merits. The first avoids the long soprano sequence of 'Rejoice greatly, O daughter of Zion' and 'He shall feed his flock', all in B flat; the second provides the alto soloist with an important air in Part Three.

The names scribbled down in this copy of the word-book give us our best information about the men soloists. There is 'Bailey' who sang tenor items; 'Mason' who sang the bass items, except 'Why do the nations so furiously rage together?' which is marked 'Hill'; 'Ward', an alto, who sang 'Then shall be brought to pass' and shared the duet 'O death, where is thy sting?' with Bailey; and 'Lamb' whose name is against 'Behold, a virgin shall conceive'—meaning, one takes for granted, that he also sang 'O thou that tellest good tidings to Zion'—and the pair of recitatives 'He that dwelleth in heaven' and 'Thou shalt break them'. These two recits are, of course, for tenor. Perhaps the writer of these names made a mistake here; on the other hand it is certainly far from impossible that the singer of 'Behold, a virgin shall conceive' also sang those.

All these singers were members of one or both of the Dublin cathedral choirs:

James Baily(s)	
William Lambe	Christ Church and
Joseph Ward	St Patrick's
John Hill	
John Mason	Christ Church

The name 'Mclean' (Mrs Maclaine) is noted against a few soprano items, but there is no mention of Signora Avolio. This makes one think that the owner of our word-book may have made his notes at the second performance, when perhaps Mrs Maclaine took Avolio's place. The newspaper report leaves no doubt that Avolio sang at the first performance.

Handel took with him to Ireland the fair manuscript copy of the score made by J. C. Smith. From now on we may conveniently refer to this as his 'conducting score'. It was Handel's practice to pencil in the names of the singers of each movement for his various performances. To this day the names of 'Baley', 'Hill', 'Ward' and 'Masson' can be made out in his hand-writing—a directly surviving link with the composer himself at Dublin, in the 'Musick Hall' at Fishamble street, in the year 1742.

This, then, is an outline of what we know, or may reasonably infer, about the earliest performances of *Messiah*, when the soloists included an Italian soprano, an English tragic actress, an organist's wife of whom nothing else whatever is known, and a group of men from the Dublin cathedrals. And it will be noted that if *Messiah* in its original form differs from what we hear at the present time, so also *Messiah* 'as it was originally performed' contains yet other, and sometimes curious, features.

Chapter IV

London

1743-5

ON his return to England, Handel cannot but have felt refreshed and encouraged by his visit to Dublin, and better able to put behind him the disappointment of his previous London season. He now added the finishing touches to *Samson* and began to form plans for another series of subscription performances. One thing was certain: it would include no opera. As it was to prove, Handel's last opera was *Deidamia*, given at the end of his 1740-41 season. In September 1742 he wrote to Jennens:

> The report that the Direction of the Opera next winter is comitted to my Care, is groundless . . . Whether i shall do something in the Oratorio way (as several of my friends desire) I can not determine as yet.[1]

But so it was to be. He announced a series of six oratorio performances to take place in Covent Garden theatre during Lent 1743, and opened with *Samson* on 18 February. This was so successful that all the remaining five performances were devoted to the same work, and an extension of the series was advertised.

If we scrutinize the announcements of these events, we shall not find any reference whatsoever to *Messiah*; however, in the newspaper for 19 March 1743, there was announced 'A New Sacred Oratorio' as the ninth event in the complete series as extended; and it was under this title that *Messiah* was first brought before the London public. It was performed at Covent Garden on 23 March, and Dubourg, who was then in London, contributed a violin solo to the proceedings, which also included an organ concerto, played, no doubt, by Handel himself.

For his women soloists Handel was able to draw on the services of Signora Avolio and Mrs Cibber who both had served him in Dublin. But he made use, besides, of two other sopranos, a Miss Edwards and Mrs Kitty Clive. The latter had a reputation as a comic actress; but she had sung the part of Dalila in *Samson* earlier in the season. From Handel's names written on his conducting score it appears that Miss Edwards, who had taken a minor part in *Samson*, sang 'I know that my redeemer liveth'. As for Mrs Clive, Handel allotted her the sequence of four 'nativity' solos, and (presumably to make her part more substantial) wrote a new setting of 'And lo, the angel of the Lord came upon them'. This displaced the well-known accompanied recitative, and took the form of an air with continuo accompaniment only, beginning thus:

Ex. 12

For men soloists there were more experienced concert singers than had been available in Dublin: John Beard sang tenor and Thomas Reinhold bass.

PLATE III

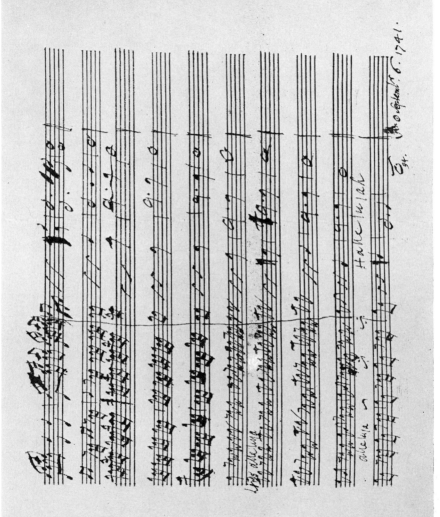

The final bars of 'Hallelujah' in the composer's autograph

PLATE IV

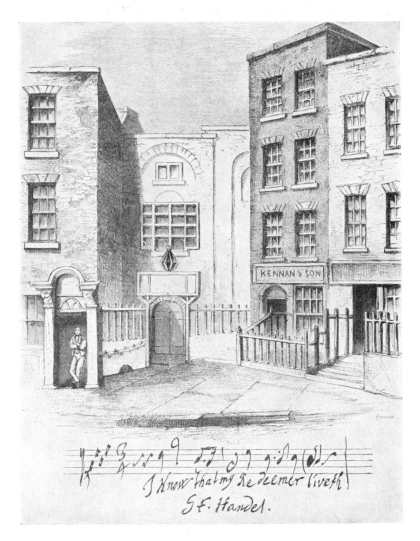

The Music Hall, Fishamble-street, Dublin
Print (after a coloured drawing by F. W. Fairholt, c. 1840)

The duet and chorus version of 'How beautiful are the feet' (the Isaiah text) as performed in Dublin was retained, but Handel rescued the words 'Their sound is gone out' by writing a short solo setting of them in F major with continuo accompaniment only. Its opening phrase is worth noting for comparison with the chorus setting, as yet not composed:

Ex. 13

Their sound is gone out ___

It was written for tenor voice, but it may be that at the last moment Handel gave it to Avolio to sing.

Apart from the retention of this duet and chorus, and the inclusion of two new settings ('And lo, the angel of the Lord came upon them', and 'Their sound is gone out') we do not know as much as we should like for certain about this performance. What happened we may wonder, about the three movements unexpectedly turned into recitatives at Dublin?

There is not much light to be shed on 'But who may abide the day of his coming?'. Yet it certainly is noteworthy that Handel did not write Reinhold's name in the conducting score on the original bass air. Perhaps this is rather negative; but as far as it goes it appears to suggest that the recitative version was used again. There is some evidence, this time of a more positive kind, that the recitative form of 'Thou shalt break them' was also sung: the copy added to the conducting score is marked 'Avolio' in Handel's writing, and as this cannot be connected with the Dublin performance it must refer to 1743, the only other year in which Avolio sang in *Messiah*. As for 'Thou art gone up on high' we do know that Handel wrote a new setting in either 1743 or 1745. This was for soprano and was 116 bars long, though both were in D minor and had the same orchestral beginning. All we can say is that perhaps this soprano setting may have been used in 1743, and this is not unreasonable when it is remembered that work had to be apportioned among no fewer than three soprano soloists. Once again it is perhaps significant that Reinhold's name is not found in the conducting score on the original bass form.

One thing, however, is certain: the work was not enthusiastically received. This is very surprising after its marked success, bordering on the sensational, in Dublin. It was *Samson* that carried all before it at Covent Garden that year, with a total of eight performances including every one of the six as first planned. Evidently, when once *Samson* had been heard, it was clear to Handel that it would not be worth while to produce *Messiah* in his first six concerts. Perhaps, when placing it third in the additional part of the season, he envisaged the possibility of three further performances. As it turned out, he repeated it only twice (25 and 29 March); and, in spite of the announcement of the seventh performance of *Samson* as 'the Last time of performing this Season' he evidently thought it wise to include yet another performance of that popular work on 31 March as the finale to his season.

Another unmistakable sign of lack of warmth is the failure of Walsh, the publisher, to issue a volume containing the overture and solos soon after the performance. It was his general custom to do this under the title of 'Songs in ———'. The appropriate publication duly and promptly appeared for *Samson*, but nothing for the 'New Sacred Oratorio'.

It is ironic to think that the chief reason for all this was probably the very factor which, in the long run, caused *Messiah* to achieve popular pre-eminence over all Handel's other works: namely that it deals, in the language of Holy Scripture, with an exalted religious theme. A correspondent who cloaked himself under the name of 'Philalethes', and who declared himself 'a profess'd Lover of *Musick*, and in particular all Mr *Handel's Performances*' thundered thus in the *Universal Spectator* of 19 March 1743:

> An *Oratorio* either is an *Act* of *Religion*, or it is not; if it is, I ask if the *Playhouse* is a fit *Temple* to perform it in, or a Company of *Players* [a hit palpably aimed, in anticipation, at people like Susanna Cibber and Kitty Clive] fit *Ministers* of *God's Word* . . .
>
> But it seems the *Old Testament* is not to be prophan'd alone . . . but the *New* must be join'd with it, and *God* by the most *sacred* the most *merciful Name* of *Messiah*; for I'm inform'd that an Oratorio call'd by that Name has already been perform'd in *Ireland*, and is soon to be perform'd *here* . . . As to the Pretence that there are many Persons who will say their *Prayers* there [*i.e.*, in the theatre] who will not go to *Church* . . . the Assertion is *false* . . . But if the Assertion was true, are the most sacred Things, *Religion* and the *Holy Bible*, which is the *Word* of *God*, to be prostituted to the perverse Humour of a Set of obstinate People . . .?[2]

When we recall Handel's advertisement of a 'New Sacred Oratorio' and how he now avoided the title *Messiah* which had been freely used in Dublin, it becomes evident that he was aware of the danger of offending such susceptibilities as 'Philalethes' so pungently expressed. It seems that these opinions had a large following and in great measure accounted for the lack of success of the oratorio on its production in London. There is no doubt that the reputation of actors and actresses for loose morals (which reputation endured in the minds of some people up to fifty years ago and was partly responsible for strenuous objections to the 'Three Choirs' festivals) was a far stronger element in this point of view that we can dream of today. To what extent the music itself was not immediately acceptable is hard to say. The fourth Earl of

Shaftesbury, in some manuscript recollections written down in 1760, appeared to think it was a union of the two factors that lay behind the relative failure. His succinct words perhaps sum the matter up:

> But partly from the Scruples, some Persons had entertained, against carrying on such a Performance in a Play House, and partly for not entering into the genius of the Composition, this Capital Composition, was but indifferently relish'd.[3]

So Handel laid *Messiah* aside and did not include it in his next year's Lenten season. However, in spite of those who thought like 'Philalethes', there were some who were more interested in the music than in any alleged impropriety. The society called the 'Academy of Antient Musick' took it up and gave a performance in February 1744, boldly announced without any beating about the bush as 'Messiah. A Sacred Oratorio'.

This society met at the Crown and Anchor tavern, at that time standing in the Strand opposite St Clement's church. One of the moving spirits was an amateur musician named Henry Needler, and he may have been the intermediary between Handel and the society. Needler, who in professional life was Accountant-general of the Excise, led the orchestra at the meetings. On his death in 1760, among his possessions was a manuscript score of *Messiah* in his handwriting. This is now in the British Museum. In all probability he was able to get access to the music through this performance by the Academy. It is not surprising that his copy includes the duet and chorus form of 'How beautiful are the feet' and the aria forms of 'And lo, the angel of the Lord came upon them' and 'Their sound is gone out'. As for 'But who may abide the day of his coming?' and 'Thou shalt break them', his copy gives the aria version of the original manuscript. Supposing that these had not been included in Handel's performances in 1743, then it may possibly be that the

Academy's performance of 1744 was the first time they were sung.

Another sign that interest in *Messiah* was not wholly lacking is found in a letter from Mrs Delany (née Mary Granville) to her sister Ann, Mrs Dewes, towards the end of the 1744 Lenten oratorio season. She expresses her hope and expectation that *Messiah* (which she refers to thus) might be the subject of the last concert. This was not so, however; and in a subsequent letter Mrs Delany laments: 'Last night, alas! was the last night of the oratorio: it concluded with Saul: I was in hopes of the Messiah'.[4] It must be said that such enthusiasm came in this instance from the party known to be attached to the composer: the Granville family was on intimate terms with Handel.

At length the composer himself determined to revive the work in his 1744-5 season. This was ambitiously conceived.Not confined to Lent, it began in November 1744 and was planned to include 24 performances, on Saturdays at first, changing to Wednesdays and Fridays in Lent. Handel now moved from Covent Garden to the King's Theatre, Haymarket. He made a particular point of securing Mrs Cibber, who promised to come if it did not conflict with her appearances at Covent Garden. She was able to join him in January, and though indisposed at the first night of *Hercules* she was able to sing in the second performance on 12 January.

Unfortunately, trouble was looming, for the season was not going well. After only six performances, Handel felt his losses were so heavy, during no more than a quarter of the season, that he could not proceed. He therefore announced that he must stop short, and offered to refund three-quarters of the amount of subscriptions received. This had the effect of rallying his well-wishers, with the result that although Handel could not carry out all his projected season, he said he felt he owed it to them to do what he could. In the end he managed a total of 16 concerts. Of these, the 14th and 16th (9 and 11 April) were devoted to 'The [or 'A'] Sacred Oratorio'.

Beard and Reinhold again took part. 'And lo, the angel of the Lord came upon them', 'How beautiful are the feet' and 'Their sound is gone out' were performed in the same versions as in 1743. But this time a singer known as 'La Francesina' was the only soprano, though she may have been assisted by a boy treble. She was a French girl whose real name was Elisabeth Duparc and who achieved a reputation as a dancer under the designation of 'La Francesina' or—by Italian approximation—Signora Francesina.

The names scrawled by Handel on his conducting score show that she sang at least the 'nativity' group, 'Behold, and see if there be any sorrow' and 'I know that my redeemer liveth'. It is possible that a boy contributed 'Rejoice greatly, O daughter of Zion'. Surprisingly, Francesina's name is found against 'He was despised', which must have been transposed for her.

Miss Robinson, the daughter of the organist of Westminster Abbey, sang contralto. Her name is found on 'Behold, a virgin shall conceive' (hence she would also sing 'O thou that tellest good tidings to Zion'). The fact that both 'Robinson' and 'Sigra Francesina' are written on the original all-soprano form of the sequence 'Then shall the eyes of the blind/He shall feed his flock' may point to the division of this, for the first time, between contralto and soprano in the way familiar to modern audiences.

From all this it rather seems that Mrs Cibber did not, after all, take part in *Messiah* this year, whether at one or both performances. But if she did, it is at this point that she leaves our story. Of all who took part in the early performances, it was she whose singing left the deepest impression. In particular, she was so identified with 'He was despised' that it came to be said this movement 'was written for her'. However that may be, and though she had but little vocal endowment ('a girl without ever a note' was Horace Walpole's acid comment), Burney felt able to say, long afterwards, that he believed this movement, notwithstanding it had since been sung by Italian singers of the greatest abilities, had never yet been given

> in a manner so truly touching to an Englishman, as by Mrs Cibber,

and though her voice was 'a mere thread' and her knowledge of music 'inconsiderable', yet

> by a natural pathos, and perfect conception of the words, she often penetrated the heart, when others, with infinitely greater skill, could only reach the ear.[5]

And of Handel's relations with her, Burney remarked:

> He was very fond of Mrs Cibber, whose voice and manners had softened his severity for her want of musical knowledge.[6]

It was about this time that copies of *Messiah* slowly began to multiply. The furnishing of these was in the hands of J. C. Smith, who either wrote them out himself or had them made by his assistants. Such a copy would be required by the Academy of Antient Musick. A splendid example in Smith's writing was acquired by Bernard Granville, brother of Mrs Delany and Mrs Dewes; this is now in the British Museum. Another, with a few pages only in Smith's handwriting, was made for someone unknown; it eventually belonged to Sir William Sterndale Bennett, the nineteenth-century composer, whose family continues to treasure it. A third copy, written by Smith in the oblong format associated with practical use rather than a library copy, was owned by William Hayes, an eighteenth-century professor of music at Oxford; this later belonged to Otto Goldschmidt, husband of Jenny Lind, and is now believed to be in America. A further one was presented by Handel late in 1743, on request, to that same Charitable Musical Society in Dublin for which the work had been first performed. This copy cannot now be traced. There is reason to think that, besides the conducting score, a copy was written out, corresponding generally to the form in which the oratorio was given in 1743-5, to serve as a master copy for making such transcripts as these. It seems probable that it was this hypothetical copy which provided the material, years later, for the earliest printed editions.

All these 'secondary' copies agree in including the aria forms of 'And lo, the angel of the Lord came upon them' and 'Their sound is gone out' as well as the duet and chorus version of 'How beautiful are the feet'. They agree also in the inclusion of the soprano version of 'Thou art gone up on high'. What we may term the makeshift recitatives do not appear; but it is not surprising that these did not circulate. None of the copies mentioned includes versions composed later than 1745, for example, the chorus setting of 'Their sound is gone out'.

Apparently the oratorio was now beginning to live down the prejudice against it, though still there was no sign of any publication by Walsh. In a long panegyric 'Ode to Mr Handel' published in May 1745, the anonymous author refers (specifically, by means of footnotes to his verses) to *Messiah* thus:

> Tremendous theme of song! the theme of love
> And melting mercy HE, when sung to strains,
>   Which from prophetic lips
>   Touch'd with ethereal fire,
>
> Breath'd balmy Peace, yet breathing in the charm
> Of healing sounds; fit prelude to the pomp
>   Of choral energy,
>   Whose lofty accents rise

To speak MESSIAH's names; the God of Might,
The Wond'rous and the Wise—the Prince of Peace.
    Him, feeder of the flock
And leader of the lambs,

The tuneful tenderness of trilling notes
Symphonious speaks: Him pious pity paints
    In mournful melody
    The man of sorrows; grief

Sits heavy on his soul, and bitterness
Fills deep his deadly draught—He deigns to die—
    The God who conquers Death,
    When, bursting from the Grave,

Mighty he mounts, and wing'd with rapid winds,
Thro' Heav'ns wide portals opening to their Lord,
    To boundless realms return'd,
    The King of Glory reigns.

Pow'rs, dominations, thrones resound HE REIGNS,
High Hallelujah's of empyreal hosts,
    And pealing Praises join
    The thunder of the spheres.[7]

Nevertheless, one notable carping voice was to be heard, that of Jennens, who, in a letter of August 1745, opined of *Messiah* that Handel had

> made a fine Entertainment of it, tho' not near so good as he might & ought to have done. I have with great difficulty made him correct some of the grossest faults in the composition, but he retain'd his Overture obstinately, in which there are some passages far unworthy of Handel, but much more unworthy of the Messiah.[8]

The less said about that expression of opinion the better.

Chapter V

Renewal and Consolidation
1749-53

IT is plain there was no regular form of *Messiah* so far
as we have yet traced its story. The first performance
differed from the work as originally composed; the
London performances of 1743-5 differed from both.
When, after a silence of three seasons, Handel at last
determined to revive the work in 1749, it is not
surprising that he made further changes in it; nor was
1749 the latest year of revisions. But after reviewing
the years 1749-53, one has a clear impression that the
changes of that period amounted to something more
than simply another variety of versions: one senses
also a degree of quickened vitality and invigoration
not noticeable earlier.

The 1749 season included, it is true, no more than a
single performance of *Messiah*; but it was now boldly
billed under its proper title. From then on, there was
never to be another year in Handel's life when it was
not to be heard in London under his direction. He
now reverted to the original, accompanied recitative
version of 'And lo, the angel of the Lord came upon
them', abandoning the aria written for Mrs Clive, and
never, so far as we know, returning to it. He also
gave up the duet and chorus setting of the Isaiah
text of 'How beautiful are the feet' and its pendant
aria 'Their sound is gone out'. Going back to his
original version, he rescued from it the first 24 bars
of the soprano aria to the Romans text, so creating
the setting of 'How beautiful are the feet' best known
today (12-8 time in G minor). Then, in place of the
remainder of the original form of that aria (to the
words 'Their sound is gone out'), he wrote the well-

known chorus to that part of the text. It is interesting
to find in his score of this chorus, written a number of
years after the original score, that Handel took the
trouble to write his own oboe parts, in which respect
this movement stands alone in *Messiah*.

A third change was in the re-casting of 'Rejoice
greatly, O daughter of Zion'. This was done in two
stages. First the composer drastically altered the plan
of his 12-8 version by making important 'cuts' and
writing a short link-passage to effect a suitable join.
As a result the aria now had 108 bars and was no
longer in *da capo* form. At this point one must recall
what has already been noted, namely that in its
original state *the bass of the* 12-8 *version was expressed in
common time*. This led to the second stage of Handel's
re-casting: above the common-time bass of this revised
form he re-wrote the soprano solo and the instrumental part in common time, thus giving the movement
more brilliant semiquaver movement in place of the
former triplets.

Each of these changes involved the soprano soloist
who now, for the first time, was Giulia Frasi. Young
and good-looking, she had, as Burney says, 'a sweet and
clear voice, and a smooth and chaste style of singing,
which, though cold and unimpassioned, pleased
natural ears, and escaped the censure of critics'.[1] One
point very much in her favour was that she could sing
well in English. Burney gives us an amusing glimpse
of her and Handel together:

> When Frasi told him, that she should study hard, and was
> going to learn Thorough-Base, in order to accompany her-
> self: HANDEL, who well knew how little this pleasing
> singer was addicted to application and diligence, says, 'Oh—
> vaat may we not expect!'.[2]

Frasi may not have been a very intelligent singer;
but the mere fact that, whether in London or the
provinces, she was regularly and continuously associa-

ted with *Messiah* from 1749 until several years after Handel's death is assurance enough of the satisfaction she must have given.

The contralto soloist was Caterina Galli, another singer new to *Messiah* this year. She and Frasi shared 'He shall feed his flock' in the familiar way. Unlike Frasi, Galli sang for Handel only until 1754. But of all who took part in *Messiah* under the composer's direction, she was the longest lived. She first gained celebrity in 1747 by her singing of 'Tis liberty alone' (*Judas Maccabaeus*), which created something of a sensation. As late as 1797, after the age of seventy and in great poverty, she appeared at Covent Garden. Lord Mount Edgecumbe noted in his 'Musical Reminiscences' (published in 1834) how her aged voice was cracked and trembling, but he also observed 'the animation and delight with which she seemed to hear again the music in which she had formerly been a distinguished performer'. This is a pathetic picture of the last years of one whose name so frequently occurs in Handel's own writing on his conducting score. She died in 1804.

At the time of his 1749 season Handel parted company, for the time being, with Beard, and in his place employed Thomas Lowe as tenor. Reinhold survived as the only link with the 1743-5 performances. Once more it is uncertain what happened about 'But who may abide the day of his coming?', but for my part I have little doubt that the recitative version did duty again. The 1749 performance—given at Covent Garden on 23 March—was unusual in that Handel seems to have employed only four soloists.

In 1750 Handel promoted a further performance on his own account. What makes the year specially notable, however, is that it saw the beginning of the charitable performances at the Foundling Hospital.

This charity for the care of orphan children (known

today as the Thomas Coram Foundation, after its founder) had already enlisted Handel's sympathies, so that when the question of a musical performance to signalize the opening of a new chapel was discussed, the sub-committee appointed for the purpose felt able to approach him on the subject. His response was generous in the extreme. To an offer to present an organ to the chapel he added a further offer to open the organ in person and to give a performance of *Messiah* on the same occasion. The date of 1 May was fixed, the performance to take place at noon.

When the day came the attendance was larger than had been expected. Tickets had been appropriately restricted to the accommodation available (ladies and gentlemen being asked to come without hoops and swords respectively); nevertheless, many people turned up hoping to pay for tickets on the spot, and in the confusion some of the ticket-holders themselves were kept out. Handel thereupon offered a further performance so that, to save embarrassment, all the original ticket-holders might be accommodated; this took place on 15 May. The new organ, one may add, was not ready in time for either performance.

This renewed association between *Messiah* and charity was decisive in the fortunes of the work. Thenceforward its popularity was ensured. It must have been from now that, as Sir John Hawkins put it,

> at length a change of sentiment in the public began to manifest itself; the Messiah was received with universal applause.[3]

Elsewhere Hawkins further says that *Messiah*:

> was frequently performed to such audiences, as he could no otherwise accommodate than by erecting seats on the stage, to such a number as scarcely left room for the performers.[4]

Each year until Handel's death the oratorio was performed in the Foundling Chapel for the benefit of the Hospital, in addition to performances given on his own account. It need hardly be said that these events constituted a most valuable source of income for the charity. In 1753, for example, the performance brought in the net sum of £496 and this rose to £607 17s 6d in 1754. It is pleasing to find that Handel's generosity was recognized by his election to the Court of Governors in May 1750.

Another feature which makes the year 1750 stand out is the appearance of a new *Messiah* singer in the person of the male alto, Gaetano Guadagni. He first came over to England as a member of an Italian troupe of comic singers which also included Frasi. His singing was at first not very cultivated, but Handel seems to have been attracted to him and engaged him for the 1750 oratorio season, when he sang not only in *Messiah* but also in *Theodora* and *Samson*. His engagement was the occasion for the composition of new versions of two movements in *Messiah*, namely, 'But who may abide the day of his coming?' and 'Thou art gone up on high'. On the sheets on which he composed these alto versions, Handel wrote in ink 'for Guadagni'. As with the common-time version of 'Rejoice greatly, O daughter of Zion', the original autographs of these movements were incorporated into Handel's conducting score, where they still are. (To make matters quite clear, this alto version of 'But who may abide the day of his coming?' composed for Guadagni, is the one containing the *prestissimo* sections to the words 'for he is like a refiner's fire'. Prout, in his edition, correctly allotted this to the alto voice; but for reasons best known to themselves, many conductors today have it sung by a bass.) About this time Handel also marked 'O death, where is thy sting?' in his conducting score, reducing it to 24 bars.

In my larger book I have given reasons why I consider Handel employed six soloists for *Messiah* in 1750—Frasi and a boy; Galli and Guadagni;

Lowe; Reinhold. Whether this applies both to the
Covent Garden and also the Foundling Hospital
performances we have no direct evidence; but it
seems not unreasonable to imagine that when offering
to perform for charity on 1 May Handel intended to
use the same versions as at his own performance
on 12 April. As I suggest, Galli sang 'O thou that
tellest good tidings to Zion' and 'O death, where is
thy sting?' as well as 'If God be for us' in the transposed
(C minor) version. To Guadagni, in addition to the
items newly composed for him, were allotted 'He
shall feed his flock' and 'He was despised'. Of the
soprano part, the boy treble took the four 'nativity'
recitatives and also the second pair of the 'passion'
solos, that is, 'He was cut off out of the land of the
living' and 'But thou didst not leave his soul in hell'.
Frasi sang the rest of the usual soprano part, together
with 'Thy rebuke hath broken his heart' and 'Behold,
and see if there be any sorrow'.

Guadagni sang for Handel again in 1751 and 1753.
In the latter year he seems to have taken the entire alto
role, including a recomposed version of the aria 'How
beautiful are the feet' in C minor (like the G minor
aria, this led to the chorus 'Their sound is gone out').
On his first arrival in England his singing was not
very polished, and Burney (who gave him some
lessons) describes it as 'wild and careless'. Yet there
must have been something in it to arrest Handel's
attention, and to judge by 'But who may abide the day
of his coming?' his voice must have been not only
flexible but powerful. After Handel's death he returned to England and made a new career for himself
singing soprano parts. But to revert to the period
under discussion, in the year 1752 when Guadagni
was away in Ireland, Galli sustained all the alto part,
including the two arias written for Guadagni in 1750.
It is therefore not necessary to think that 'But who

may abide the day of his coming?' must always be
sung by a *male* alto. And both the original (bass)
version and the recitative now finally give place to the
latest version for alto.

There is one other interesting variant version which
appears to be associated with the earlier 1750's and
that is the shortened form of 'Why do the nations so
furiously rage together?' in which the later part ('The
Kings of the earth rise up . . .') is set as a brief recitative.
Handel's autograph of this recitative portion is yet
another item incorporated as an addition to his conducting score. One authority, Professor J. P. Larsen,
has suggested that in the first instance this was used in
Dublin in 1742, but for myself I cannot feel there is
particular evidence to that effect. Nevertheless, this
version certainly goes back to the early years of
Messiah history, and it was also in use in the earlier
1750's. Some listeners may indeed be disappointed by
such cutting short of a favourite 'aria infuriata',
although it seems to me to have undoubted merit of
its own in the way it moves forward swiftly, with
dramatic intent, to 'Let us break their bonds asunder'.

Beard came back into Handel's cast in 1752, never
again to forsake it. Reinhold died in 1751. There are
very strong grounds for assuming that from 1750 the
bass role never varied (unless it be between the two
forms of 'Why do the nations so furiously rage
together?') and it passed to two less distinguished
singers, Wass and Champness, for the rest of Handel's
life.

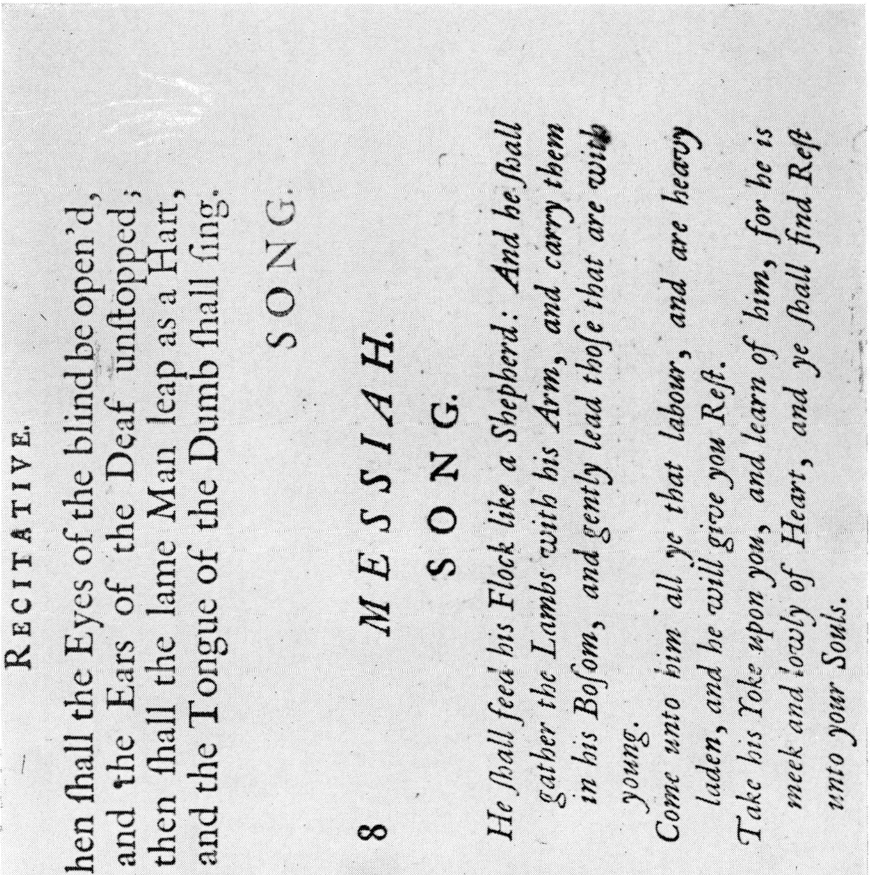

PLATE V

RECITATIVE.

Then ſhall the Eyes of the blind be open'd,
and the Ears of the Deaf unſtopped;
then ſhall the lame Man leap as a Hart,
and the Tongue of the Dumb ſhall ſing.

SONG.

MESSIAH.

SONG.

8

He ſhall feed his Flock like a Shepherd: And he ſhall
gather the Lambs with his Arm, and carry them
in his Boſom, and gently lead thoſe that are with
young.
Come unto him all ye that labour, and are heavy
laden, and he will give you Reſt.
Take his Yoke upon you, and learn of him, for he is
meek and lowly of Heart, and ye ſhall find Reſt
unto your Souls.

Contemporary annotations (1749, 1752, 1753) to a word-book printed in 1749

PLATE VI

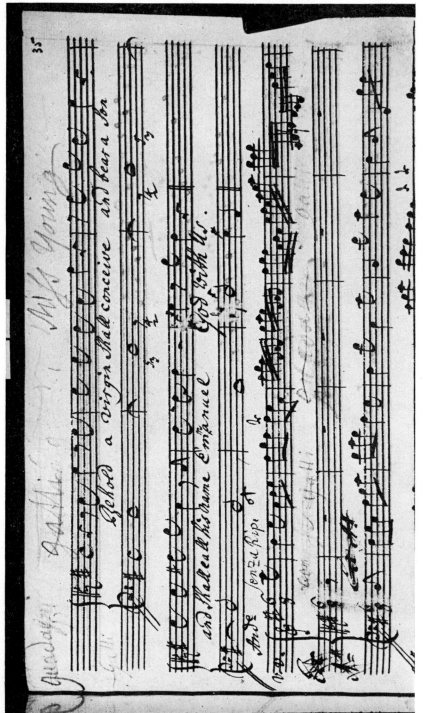

Singers' names written by Handel on 'Behold, a virgin shall conceive' in his conducting score

Chapter VI

The Foundling Hospital performance of 1754:
Handel's last years

WHAT remains to be told of *Messiah* during the last six years of Handel's life probably might not justify a separate chapter were it not for the survival of details, so full as to be well-nigh comprehensive, about the performance in the Foundling Hospital on 15 May 1754. These are so interesting that they must be summarized in the first part of this chapter, before we turn to some information about other aspects of *Messiah* history up to and including the year of Handel's death.

The number of tickets sold for the Foundling Hospital in 1754 was 1,219. The orchestra consisted of fifteen violins, five violas, three cellos, two double basses, four bassoons and four oboes, with two trumpets and the drums; in addition, somewhat to our surprise, there were two horns. The hornists must have shared the trumpet parts in 'Hallelujah' and 'Worthy is the Lamb', playing an octave lower. For chorus, there were six trebles from the Chapel Royal and thirteen men divided among the alto, tenor, and bass parts. The soloists, five in number, also assisted in the choruses. Handel's pupil, J. C. Smith the younger (son of the copyist and man-of-affairs to Handel), was the organist.

There were two soprano soloists. One of them, Signora Passerini, had a most interesting role: to her Handel allotted transposed versions of the 'Guadagni' settings of 'But who may abide the day of his coming?' and 'Thou art gone up on high' as well as the original,

untransposed version of 'If God be for us'. Thus she
had a substantial aria, of brilliant, ringing character, in
each of the three Parts of the oratorio. It must have
been thrilling to hear 'But who may abide the day of
his coming?' a fifth higher (that is in A minor) than it
was originally written for Guadagni.

Frasi retained all the rest of the usual soprano
numbers, singing 'He shall feed his flock' in its
original, all-soprano form, and taking also 'He was
cut off out of the land of the living' and 'But thou
didst not leave his soul in hell'. With the exception of
these two numbers, Beard sang all the tenor solos.
The alto role, now shorn of 'But who may abide the
day of his coming?' and 'Thou art gone up on high',
was sustained by Galli. Wass was the bass soloist, and
his part included the form of 'Why do the nations so
furiously rage together?' with the recitative ending.

In the 'Pastoral Symphony' Handel returned to his
original short form, that is to say the first eleven bars
only, treating it rather as a lifting of the curtain on the
nativity scene which follows than as an independent
short orchestral piece. 'Their sound is gone out' took
the chorus form, preceded by the short soprano aria
'How beautiful are the feet'.

There is a great deal of food for thought in these
details. This was certainly not the only form in which
Handel gave Messiah, even after his important revisions
of 1749-50. In that sense it cannot be thought of as
finally definitive. Yet it is the one performance of
which we know every version without doubt and for
which we have exact knowledge of how the solo work
was divided. If we perform it in this way—and very
effective it is—we may be sure of following the plan of
at least one of Handel's own performances.

One notes also the small scale of the resources
employed. There was no monster chorus to blur the
contrapuntal outline, blunt the edge of the florid

divisions and swamp the orchestral detail, and no large body of strings to make four oboes inaudible; but the instrumental bass was strongly reinforced by four bassoons. This choral-orchestral scale and balance is confirmed by details which also survive about the Foundling Hospital performances of 1758 and 1759.

From 1753 Handel, to all intents and purposes, was blind, though still able, no doubt, to write his name. Perhaps it was on this account, soon after the 1754 performance, that the Governors of the Foundling Hospital took it on themselves to consult Handel, considering 'that it may be very proper to put such Performances under proper Regulations'.[1] As a result, Handel appointed his pupil Smith, now organist of the Foundling chapel, to conduct, and 'on Account of his Health he excused himself from giving any further Instructions relating to the Performances'. This has been taken to mean that 1754 was the last year he conducted in person at the Hospital. But it would seem that his spirits revived and he resumed his part. Not only did he do so in 1757, but the advertisement, issued shortly before his death, of the performance planned for 3 May 1759 announced that it would be 'under the Direction of *George-Frederick Handel* Esq.'[2] In the event, Handel died in the interval between advertisement and performance, which had to be conducted by the younger Smith.

The extent of Handel's conspicuous generosity towards the Foundling Hospital appears to have been misunderstood, though no doubt in good faith, by the Governors, who were under the impression that he intended them to have the *exclusive* rights to the work after his death. This would have required parliamentary enactment, and accordingly a draft petition was drawn up in 1754. There is a well-known anecdote of Handel's stormy outburst when this proposal reached his ears; but the Minutes of the Hospital cover the affair blandly by recording 'the same did not seem agreeable to Mr Handel for the present.'³ And so the matter rested. Nevertheless, Handel's intention remained firm that the Hospital should continue to benefit from the work after his death, and by a clause in the third codicil to his Will (dated 4 August 1757) he bequeathed 'a fair copy of the Score and all Parts of my Oratorio called The Messiah to the Foundling Hospital'.

The manuscripts still belong to the Foundation. Handel's executors duly had them copied to carry out the terms of the Will, and they were handed over by the younger Smith on 13 June. It so happens that they had the parts copied from those used at the 1754 performance, and that is one of the reasons we know so much about it. This Foundling Hospital material was quite evidently derived, in the long run, from Handel's conducting score, which had been kept up-to-date by the revisions from 1749 onwards. So it is that the Foundling Hospital manuscripts are considerably different from those mentioned in an earlier chapter, associated with the names of Granville, Sterndale Bennett, and Goldschmidt. For the same reason they are different from the earliest printed editions, which, though they did not appear until after Handel's death, can be traced back to some copy made before the changes of 1749-50. The Foundling Hospital manuscripts include parts for oboes and bassoons.

No new version of any movement was written after 1753. Possibly the latest was the alto (C minor) form of 'How beautiful are the feet' which we associate with Guadagni. Thereafter variety was introduced into Messiah by reviving older versions, or by transpositions for other voices. Thus, the original short form of the 'Pastoral Symphony' was used, as we have seen, and the G minor form of 'How beautiful are the feet'. There is, however, no sign that Mrs Clive's aria 'And lo, the angel of the Lord came upon them' was ever revived, or any setting of 'But who may abide the day of his coming?' and 'Thou art gone up on high' earlier than Guadagni's. Nor can I see convincing evidence that any other form of 'Rejoice greatly, O daughter of Zion' than the common-time one was used after 1749, though I say this with regret: for, as a subjective, not historical, judgment, I prefer the 12-8 version *in its abbreviated form* to any other. There is some possibility that towards the end of his life Handel sanctioned a revival of the duet and chorus setting of 'How beautiful are the feet' (Isaiah text).

Frasi and Beard continued as regular soloists, but after 1754 Galli's name disappears. In her place a new star arose, Isabella Young (later Mrs Scott) who took over the alto role including the two numbers composed in 1750 for Guadagni. A few years later Miss Young (after her marriage she used both her names indifferently) became a much sought-after singer, requiring very high fees. At the Foundling Hospital performance of 1758 she shared the alto part with Cassandra Frederick, but sang alone in 1759. There was a novelty in 1759 in the shape of Signor Ricciarelli (soprano), who sang beside Signora Frasi. His name is found (not, of course, written by Handel) in the conducting score on 'But who may abide the day of his coming?' and 'Thou art gone up on high' (Guadagni's version); perhaps, then, his voice was really of alto range.

In each of the years 1754-58 *Messiah* was given once at the Foundling Hospital after having received one, two or three performances at Covent Garden. In 1758 the Academy of Antient Musick gave a further performance of its own; this may not have included any of the post-1744 revisions, since it seems likely from the word-book that the material of the Academy's earlier performance was still in use.

In 1759 there were three Covent Garden performances, on 30 March, 4 and 6 April. In spite of ill-health, Handel appears to have attended them all, certainly the last, which brought his season to its close as planned. But on 11 April he executed a fourth codicil to his Will, remembering in it 'Mr Mathew Dubourg Musician'. There was some intention that he should go to Bath for the waters, but he was by now too ill to undertake the journey. In the morning of 14 April he died. The *Whitehall Evening Post* that day reported:

> When he went home from the Messiah Yesterday Se'nnight, he took to his Bed, and has never rose from it since; and it was with great Difficulty he attended his Oratorios at all, having been in a very bad State of Health for some Time before they began.[4]

So *Messiah* was the last thing he performed; and he died on the morrow of the 17th anniversary of its first performance.

Chapter VII

Outside London

1743-59

THE slow headway made by *Messiah* during its early years in London was reflected, not unnaturally, in the way it was gradually taken up elsewhere. As might be expected, the Irish capital was an exception to this. A performance in Dublin, under Dubourg's direction, was advertised for December 1743. This was postponed; but what had at first been planned as a single performance became two, one for the Charitable Musical Society (for relief of those in prison for debt), the other for the Infirmary on the Inn's Quay, both of which had shared in the proceeds when the work was first given in 1742. These two performances were the earliest of all those neither promoted nor conducted by the composer. They were held in the first home of *Messiah*, the Music Room in Fishamble Street, and were based on a manuscript score which Handel had provided for the purpose towards the end of 1743. One would like to know more about this: how far did it conform, one wonders, to his London performances earlier that same year? When *Messiah* was next given in Dublin, in 1745, we do know that it included not only the duet and chorus 'How beautiful are the feet' but also the aria 'Their sound is gone out' which originated in London in 1743. But, curiously enough, the 1745 Dublin performance did not also include Mrs Clive's 1743 aria form of 'And lo, the angel of the Lord came upon them'; wisely (as one might think) the Dubliners preferred the original accompanied recitative version which Handel had personally used in 1742.

Dublin remained faithful to the work, in one form or another, and it was subsequently performed there on no fewer than six more occasions during Handel's lifetime, and generally for charity.

The earliest English provincial performance that has been traced was at Oxford, where William Hayes, the professor of music, was an ardent Handelian. When the Radcliffe Camera was formally opened in April 1749 he organized three concerts of Handel's music, the third of which, held in the Sheldonian Theatre, consisted of *Messiah* under the title of 'The Sacred Oratorio'. The word-book indicates that this was based on Handel's own performances of 1743; one may be sure it did not include his revisions for the London performance on 23 March 1749. Passing over another Oxford performance of which we know little and which may not have been organized by Hayes, we find that for the Commemoration of Founders and Benefactors of 1754 the professor again arranged three Handelian concerts, *Messiah* being the third (5 July). For this he had an ambitious number of performers—'near an Hundred' said the *Oxford Journal*—obtaining instrumentalists from London and including Frasi, Beard, and Wass among the soloists. This was followed by annual performances in Oxford from 1755, either in the Sheldonian Theatre or the Holywell Music Room.

Meanwhile, probably through Handel's friend James Harris (author of 'Hermes') who lived at Salisbury, the work was introduced there. At that time there was a musical festival based on the cathedral but including evening concerts in the Assembly Hall. At one of these *Messiah* was given on 4 October 1750, no doubt under the direction of John Stephens, the cathedral organist. The work was referred to as 'The

Messiah, or Sacred Oratorio'. There seems to have been a total of rather more than thirty performers, vocalists and instrumentalists together. The *Salisbury Journal*, with local pride, speaking not only of *Messiah* but of all the music of the festival, said it 'was performed with great Exactness throughout, and in many parts with great Elegance',[1] and recorded that there were over 400 people in the audiences for the evening concerts.

The next time *Messiah* occurred at Salisbury, in the festival of 1752, parts of it were given not at an evening concert in a secular hall but actually as part of the morning festival events in the cathedral. This may not seem in any way exceptionable now, but it must be borne in mind that such morning events, as at similar festivals at Gloucester, Hereford, and Worcester, were strictly 'cathedral services', consisting of *Te Deum*, *Jubilate* and one or more anthems, all on a large scale and with orchestral accompaniment but within the framework of the Book of Common Prayer. *Messiah* was fitted into this scheme by an innocent device, best indicated in the report of the *Salisbury Journal*:

> The Anniversary Musical Festival was celebrated here on the 27th and 28th instant [September]. The Musick in the Cathedral Church on the first day began with an Overture, then followed a Te Deum set for Voices and Instruments, then an Anthem taken from the first and second Acts of the Messiah or Sacred Oratorio; and at the conclusion of the Service the famous Coronation Anthem of God save the King [the conclusion of Handel's 'Zadok the Priest']. On the second day a different Overture, the same Te Deum, an Anthem from the third Act of the Messiah or Sacred Oratorio; the conclusion as before, God save the King.[2]

At the Salisbury Festival this year the orchestra is known to have consisted of sixteen violins, two violas, four cellos, two double basses, two oboes and one bassoon, with horns, trumpets and drums.

There still exists today a fascinating document arising out of these early Salisbury performances. Round about 1760 one of the lay vicars-choral of the cathedral was named John Matthews. He obtained access to the vocal and orchestral parts which had been used, and from these he compiled a manuscript score for himself. He was also in touch with Winchester, where he found parts which differed somewhat from the Salisbury ones, and he was keen enough to copy the different Winchester versions into his score also. Matthews's score, it will readily be seen, was written up from parts, whereas of course the reverse was commonly the case—the score coming first and parts being drawn from it. So it happens that where scores of *Messiah* do not normally include any oboes, this one does, and we therefore know what kind of oboe parts were used at these early Salisbury performances. Perhaps they were the work of Stephens, the cathedral organist; they are certainly more interesting and less casual than the Foundling Hospital ones. They may be obtained, if desired, instead of the latter, as part of the edition for which I am responsible.

Another interesting result of the way Matthews's score originated is that, being compiled from performing parts, it includes many more indications of ornamentation than a score would ordinarily do. Here is what he copied in 'But thou didst not leave his soul in hell':

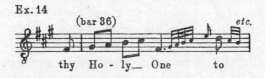

Ex. 14
(bar 36)   etc.
thy Ho - ly__ One   to

Comparing what Matthews got from Salisbury with

what he found at Winchester, the differences are as follows:

	Salisbury	Winchester
1. Rejoice greatly, O daughter of Zion	short 12-8	12-8 *da capo*
2. Then shall the eyes of the blind	alto	soprano
3. He shall feed his flock . . .	alto	soprano
. . . Come unto him	alto	soprano
4. Thou art gone up on high	original bass form	1743-5 soprano form
5. How beautiful are the feet	duet & chorus (Isaiah text)	(Romans text) *dal*
6. Their sound is gone out	aria in F major	*segno* aria
7. Why do the nations so furiously rage together?	with recit. ending	original version

Matthews noted that the 'Salisbury' versions of the first six of the items were also contained in what he called 'Mr Harris's score', but he is silent about the seventh. Of 'And lo, the angel of the Lord came upon them' he found only Mrs Clive's aria form; and of 'But who may abide the day of his coming?' only the original bass form. When he had finished copying out his score, and had it bound in December 1761, he knew nothing of the settings written for Guadagni of that and 'Thou art gone up on high'; nor was he aware of the common-time form of 'Rejoice greatly, O daughter of Zion', or of the division of 'He shall feed his flock' between alto and soprano.

Matthews later left Salisbury for Durham Cathedral, and then went on to the cathedrals of Dublin, where he died. His manuscript now belongs to Archbishop Marsh's Library there. Its survival sheds light on many things. In particular it shows how, at two provincial centres in the 1750's, the text of *Messiah*, though it differed in various ways, was alike in this: it was all derived from versions composed or transposed before 1749. 'Mr Harris' and others had obtained copies that took no account of the more recent developments, and this settled the form of Salisbury and Winchester performances in that way for many years to come.

Other towns which took up *Messiah* were Bath and Bristol. At Bath in May 1755 the soloists included Signora Passerini, who only a few days earlier had sung under the composer in London. The organizer of this event, held in 'Wiltshire's Rooms', was her husband, then settled in Bath; among those taking part was William Hayes of Oxford. The Passerini's were also associated with a further performance in Bath in November 1756 at 'Simpson's Great Room'. A two-day festival based on the Abbey Church was held in May 1759, and on the second day, in the Assembly Hall, William Hayes again conducted *Messiah*.

At Bristol 'the oratorio of Messiah' was performed in 'the New Musick Room' in January 1756, and on 17 August 1758 'The Sacred Oratorio' was given in the cathedral itself (in the evening) for the benefit of clergymen's widows and children. In the audience was John Wesley, who noted in his Journal under the same date, 'I doubt if that congregation was ever so serious at a sermon as they were during this performance. In many parts, especially several of the choruses, it exceeded my expectation.'[3] It was again performed in Bristol in August 1758.

The festivals of Gloucester, Hereford, and Worcester had long made Handel's music staple fare both in and out of the cathedrals, but *Messiah* did not appear until 1757, when it formed the final evening event at the Booth Hall in Gloucester. Again William Hayes conducted, and the singers included Frasi, Beard, and Wass. Incidentally, the word-book for this occasion—the only known copy of which belongs to Dr James S. Hall—bears the imprint of a Gloucester printer famous for his establishment of Sunday Schools: Robert Raikes.

Next year, Worcester's turn, *Messiah* was given there in College Hall, again on the last evening. The conductor is unknown. A minor poet, William Shenstone, who was present, took it on himself to observe:

> I presume, nothing in the way of harmony can possibly go further than the Oratorio of The Messiah. It seems the best composer's best composition. Yet I fancied I could observe *some parts* in it, wherein Handel's judgment failed him.[4]

The following year, 1759, Hereford extended the festival by one morning and gave *Messiah* openly in the cathedral without any pretence that it was part of a service. The conductor was Richard Clack, organist of the cathedral; this is the first year in which the resident organist conducted the festival. Thereafter, with only two exceptions (1875 and 1955) *Messiah* has invariably formed part of the Three Choirs Festival. But for these early days one must not picture the large forces used at the present time, nor the great crowd assembled in the spacious naves of the cathedrals. Until 1834 the festivals were always held in the choir, special seating being arranged to the east of the tower.

Chapter VIII

Twenty-five years on

1760-84

BY the time of Handel's death his music was already old-fashioned. The new 'galant' style was now admired by the up-to-date, and the leading figure in musical London was J. C. Bach (the 'English Bach'), whose music was to exert such an influence on the boy Mozart when he came to England only five years after Handel's death. Nevertheless, Handel still had disciples and devotees, while *Messiah*, in particular, had already begun to sink those deep roots which have ever since sustained it against the winds of changing fashions.

In promoting Lenten series of oratorios, Handel's mantle fell naturally on J. C. Smith the younger. In fact, Thomas Morell (the librettist of *Judas Maccabaeus*) in a letter written about 1764 refers to him as 'Mr Handell's successor'. To assist him, Smith obtained the services of John Stanley, the blind musician, who later continued the series (after Smith retired to Bath), with the help of Thomas Linley, up to the year 1785. Smith also directed the annual performances of *Messiah* at the Foundling Hospital from 1760 to 1768, and Stanley followed him until 1777, when for some reason they came to an end.

At the end of Handel's life his conducting score of *Messiah*, having been subject to heavy use, shewed signs of its hard wear. Either shortly before or after 1760, therefore, the elder Smith wrote out a new copy for his son's use. This contained the 'Guadagni' version of 'But who may abide the day of his coming?'

and 'Thou art gone up on high'; the 'Pastoral Symphony was the short eleven-bar form; 'Rejoice greatly, O daughter of Zion' was in common time and 'He shall feed his flock' was divided between alto and soprano; 'Why do the nations so furiously rage together?' was in the shortened form with recitative ending. Afterwards, for some particular performances, the younger Smith transposed two alto numbers for soprano and inserted them into the manuscript. They are 'But who may abide the day of his coming?' in G minor (a fourth higher) and 'He was despised' in B flat (a fifth higher).

Frasi's name is pencilled on 'Comfort ye, my people', and Guadagni's (referring to his second English period) on 'But who may abide the day of his coming?' (at the original pitch) and 'He shall feed his flock'.

In the early part of the nineteenth century this copy was found in a Bristol bookshop. It now forms part of the State-and-University Library of Hamburg. It is clearly a transcript of Handel's own conducting score, taking into account many modifications which that had undergone since it was first made, long before, by the elder Smith.

In continuing to give performances of *Messiah* the younger Smith appears to have followed Handel's practice of introducing new singers, and revising the various roles. There was, of course, no new music; but transposition was resorted to. In 1767 the renowned male soprano, Guarducci, was engaged; he had to come to England in the previous year to take part in J. C. Bach's *Caratacco*. He was allotted the following arias in *Messiah*:

Comfort ye, my people
Ev'ry valley shall be exalted
Come unto him (Mrs Scott having sung 'He shall feed his flock')

He was despised (transposed, presumably, to B flat)
Thy rebuke hath broken his heart
Behold, and see if there be any sorrow
I know that my redeemer liveth

He may well also have sung 'All they that see him laugh him to scorn'.

Frasi included the second pair of 'passion' movements ('He was cut off out of the land of the living' and 'But thou didst not leave his soul in hell') in her part, which otherwise consisted of the four 'nativity' recitatives, 'Rejoice greatly, O daughter of Zion' and 'How beautiful are the feet' (G minor aria). All that was left to the tenor soloist (a member of the Hayes family whose Christian name is not stated) was 'He that dwelleth in heaven' and 'Thou shalt break them', together with the duet 'O death, where is thy sting'. Mrs Scott had all the usual alto solos (including 'But who may abide the day of his coming?') except 'He was despised'. It will be seen how Guarducci's part was carved out of what is usually the soprano, alto and tenor parts; the bass part alone remained normal—if one may use such an expression in relation to *Messiah*. These details are derived from an interesting annotated copy of the word-book for 1767, published by Johnson, now belonging to Mr Gerald Coke.

Several other word-books survive of London performances of the 1760's, and these disclose an astonishing dispute that was conducted in their very pages. Beginning in Handel's own day, earlier word-books had carried some such imprint as:

> Printed for J. Watts: And Sold by B. Dod at the Bible and Key in Ave-Mary-Lane near Stationers-Hall.

Watts had them printed, and advertised them for sale at Dod's; and in that sense he, not Handel, was the publisher, unlike modern concert-giving bodies which usually arrange for printing and selling books of words

PLATE VII

The interior of the Foundling Hospital Chapel
Engraving by John Sanders, 1773

PLATE VIII

View of the performers at the Commemoration of Handel, 1784

themselves. A nearer modern parallel is perhaps the publication by Messrs Novello of the word-book of Elgar's *Dream of Gerontius*. Watts died in 1763, and in consequence word-books were then issued with such an imprint as that used for the 1766 *Messiah* book:

> Printed for the Administrator of J. Watts: And sold by G. Woodfall ... and S. Hooper ...

Dod ceased to be in business after 1765. In 1767 two rival publications appeared, one, as before,

> Printed for the Administrator of J. Watts

the other

> Printed for E. Johnson, Successor to the late Mr Dod.

Johnson's publication was announced as 'from a Copy corrected by the Compiler'; and it did indeed correct a long-standing error in Watts's text of 'The trumpet shall sound' and it also designated 'But who may abide the day of his coming?' and 'Thou art gone up on high' as 'Songs' where Watts had persistently headed them as 'Recitatives'.

When the next year came round, Johnson's publication included a sharply-worded 'Advertisement By the Proprietor; To whom the Compiler has given not only the entire Property of this, but also that of his other *Oratorios*, under his Signature'. (This 'Advertisement' is pasted into the British Museum copy of Johnson's issue, seeming to indicate last-minute action on getting wind of the Watts-Hooper print for that year.) It proceeds to assert that Watts's administrator had claimed that Johnson's edition was a pirated one; but Johnson states that 'the Compiler' had enjoined Watts's administrator 'to print it no more'. He does not deny that Watts himself had licence to print it; but he does imply that after Watts's death Jennens did not renew his permission to Watts's administrator, and gave it to Johnson instead. The same advertisement appears, not pasted in but as part of the original

E

printing, in Johnson's publication for 1768, and it is still found as late as 1776. The last-named issue is not only announced, like those for 1767 and 1768 as 'A New Edition. From a Copy corrected by the Compiler', but also as 'Printed, by Authority of the Compiler, for E. Johnson . . .'

What the rights and wrongs of this quarrel were—depending on Jennens's dealings with Watts in the first place—no one can now say, but Winton Dean in his book 'Handel's Dramatic Oratorios and Masques' (p. 99) tells us that the authorities at Covent Garden refused to sell the Johnson books in the theatre itself.

Meanwhile, more important events in the history of *Messiah* had been taking place than this unedifying squabble. At last the overture and solo movements appeared in print. A good deal of mystery surrounds the publication of the volume *Songs in Messiah* by John Walsh. Already we have noticed that Walsh apparently took no steps to issue such a volume in 1743 after the London première. The earliest copies known cannot have appeared before 1763: yet it has been proved beyond reasonable doubt by William C. Smith (in his book 'Concerning Handel') that *the plates from which they were printed must have been prepared about 1749*. If any were put on the market, they have not survived, and it is quite impossible to imagine that copies were on sale for as long as fourteen years (1749-63) without the survival of a single one. Moreover, no advertisement has been traced during that period. What it seems to come to is this—having, for whatever reason, failed to produce it in 1743, Walsh at last makes up his mind to do so in 1749. He goes to the trouble and expense of engraving the plates, and then for some unfathomable reason prints no copies. At last in 1763 he determines to make use of the plates, and *Songs in Messiah* at length appears.

On looking through it we find nothing composed

from 1749 onwards. It is a mixture of the form of the work as originally composed (so including the *dal segno* aria setting of 'How beautiful are the feet') and as given in London 1743-5 (including, therefore, Mrs Clive's aria 'And lo, the angel of the Lord came upon them' and the soprano D minor form of 'Thou art gone up on high'). All the versions written 1749-50, such as Guadagni's setting of 'But who may abide the day of his coming' and the common-time 'Rejoice greatly, O daughter of Zion' are excluded, as well as the original accompanied recitative 'And lo, the angel of the Lord came upon them'. It was therefore not representative of *Messiah* as it had become familiar in London in the years of its greatest popularity before the death of Handel.

It should be noted that the publication included orchestral accompaniments in score, not in an arrangement for the harpsichord or other keyboard instrument.

Walsh died in 1766, and his business was continued by William Randall and John Abell. Deeming the time ripe for a publication including the choruses, Randall and Abell placed a complete full score on the market in 1767. They used the plates of the volume *Songs in Messiah* for the overture and solo items, adding new plates for the choruses. Thus the solos have two page-numbers—first the number as in *Songs in Messiah* and second as in the complete score. At the end the publishers added a substantial Appendix containing the versions composed from 1749, together with other things such as the accompanied recitative 'And lo, the angel of the Lord came upon them'. In retrospect we possess the clues to the curious form taken by the full score; but in 1767 its publication must have given a confused notion of the work to those not directly in touch with its evolution. To take one outstanding instance, it makes it seem that the accompanied recitative 'And lo, the angel of the Lord came upon them' was a revised setting, whereas it is the original.

The various successors in business of Randall and Abell continued to publish it until the early years of the nineteenth century. Successive editions contained certain modifications, not without importance; nevertheless, they were still fundamentally the same as the 1767 publication of Randall and Abell (itself based on Walsh's *Songs in Messiah*), even up to the time when the plates eventually came into the ownership of Alfred Novello who, regrettable to relate, printed an edition from them with a spurious 'Walsh' title page. Not only was this a fake: it was based on a false assumption. Walsh never issued a complete score of *Messiah*.

Quite apart from the way the various versions were chosen and placed, both *Songs in Messiah* and the complete score in 1767 contained many inaccuracies which have bedevilled more modern editions based on them. They were not engraved from either of the conducting scores but (except for the Appendix) from a carelessly written manuscript transcribed, it would seem, in the 1740's.

Chapter IX

The Westminster Abbey Commemoration
1784

IN 1776 a group of influential admirers of the older
style of music formed what was called 'the Noble-
men's Concert of Antient Music' for the purpose of
maintaining it against the encroachment of the modern
style. The essential rule of 'the Antient Concert' (as the
organization was called for short) was that nothing
should be performed which had been composed less
than twenty years previously. Although not ex-
plicitly provided for, one of the main aims of this
institution (which survived well into the nineteenth
century) was to perpetuate Handel's music.

Three of the moving spirits of this enterprise,
Viscount Fitzwilliam, Sir Watkin Williams Wynn, and
Joah Bates, Esquire, were struck by the fact that in
1783 'the number of eminent musical performers of
all kinds, both vocal and instrumental, with which
London abounded, was far greater than in any other
city of Europe'. Accordingly, they resolved to employ
this resource in a commemoration of the birth of
Handel, which they believed to have taken place in
1684. They persuaded their fellow-directors of the
Antient Concert to manage the undertaking, and,
having previously ensured the patronage of the king
(George III), obtained permission to hold the commemoration in Westminster Abbey. The proceeds
were to be divided between the Westminster Infirmary
and the Musical Fund (now the Royal Society of
Musicians).

Two performances were projected for the Abbey,
and one for the Pantheon in Oxford Street. To these

three events there were eventually added two more in the Abbey by special request of the king and queen. *Messiah* was given twice, at the third and fifth performances. It was intended to commemorate not only Handel's birth, but also his death, by arranging that the first performance should take place in the Abbey on 21 April 1784, the twenty-fifth anniversary of his burial there. However, for more than one reason, it was eventually decided to hold the first performance on 26 May.

Preparations were made on an amazing scale. The nave of the Abbey was transformed by the architect Wyatt to provide a great auditorium after 'the effect of a royal musical chapel, with the orchestra terminating one end [the west end] and the accommodation for the Royal Family, the other.' The effect constituted

> one of the grandest and most magnificent spectacles which imagination can delineate . . . all the preparations for receiving their Majesties, and the first personages in the kingdom, at the east end; upwards of Five Hundred Musicians at the west; and the public in general, to the number of between three and four thousand persons, in the area and galleries, so wonderfully corresponded with the style of architecture of this venerable and beautiful structure, that there was nothing visible, either for use or ornament, which did not harmonize with the principal tone of the building, and which may not, metaphorically, have been said to be in *perfect tune* with it. But, besides the wonderful manner in which this construction exhibited the band to the spectators, the Orchestra was so judiciously contrived, that almost every performer, both vocal and instrumental, was in full view of the conductor and leader; which accounts, in some measure, for the uncommon ease with which the performers confess they executed their parts.[1]

The number of performers was staggering. The strings alone—forty-eight first violins, forty-seven seconds, twenty-six violas, twenty-one cellos and fifteen double basses—totalled 157, with twenty-six oboes and as many bassoons in support, and no fewer than twelve trumpets. In addition there were six flutes and twelve horns, which probably did not play in *Messiah*, and six trombones, whose players performed on other instruments when trombones were not needed. Special features, intended to give both weight and depth, were a double bassoon ('so conspicuous in the Orchestra and powerful in its effect') and three pairs of kettle drums—'double base kettle drums' specially made, the 'Tower drums' (taken at the battle of Malplaquet) and ordinary kettle drums—with four players.

The chorus was of corresponding enormity. Disregarding the principal vocalists there were fifty-three trebles (forty-seven of them boys), forty-five altos (all men), eighty tenors and seventy-nine basses, making 257 in all. To assist in 'arranging the performers, and conveying signals to the several parts of that wide-extended Orchestra' the services of Dr Samuel Arnold, Mr (later Dr) Thomas Saunders Dupuis and Mr Redmond Simpson were enlisted, 'Dr Arnold and Mr Dupuis having been placed, on different sides of the Orchestra, over the vocal choir, and Mr Simpson in the centre, over the subordinate instrumental performers' Two hundred and sixty-seven separate vocal and instrumental parts were required for *Messiah* alone.

The real wonder of the affair was the way it was directed. For this huge and wide-spread concourse of singers and players no visual beat (such as was then common for vocal, but not instrumental, music) was employed. The 'conductor', Joah Bates, directed the whole musical proceedings in the Abbey (after only one rehearsal for each performance) from a harpsichord to which there were attached communicating levers, nineteen feet long, running from the organ specially built by Samuel Green. This contrivance, we are told, required 'uncommon ingenuity and mechanical resources' in order not to render the touch impracticably heavy. Only Dr Burney's rotund phrases, one feels, can do justice to the situation:

> As this Commemoration is not only the first instance of a band of such magnitude being assembled together, but of *any* band, at all numerous, performing in a similar situation, without the assistance of a *Manu-ductor*, to regulate the measure, the performances in Westminster-Abbey may be safely pronounced, no less remarkable for the multiplicity of voices and instruments employed, than for accuracy and precision. When all the wheels of that huge machine, the Orchestra, were in motion, the effect resembled clock-work in every thing, but want of feeling and expression.[2]

Of the solo singers we need only concern ourselves with those who took part in *Messiah*. The chief doubt facing the organizers was the balance between the huge orchestra and the soloists. Fortunately at least one singer, Madam Mara, a German soprano, was fully equal to the demands of the situation, and she constituted one of the chief attractions, singing, in *Messiah*, the nativity music, 'Rejoice greatly, O daughter of Zion' (described as a 'brilliant and difficult Air'—words perhaps pointing to the common-time version), and 'I know that my redeemer liveth'. Other soprano airs were sung by Miss Cantelo and Signor Bartolini. The first pair of 'passion' movements was sung by Mr Norris, the second pair by Miss Abrams, while another tenor, Mr Harrison, sang the two opening solo numbers. 'He shall feed his flock' was divided between Signor Bartolini and Miss Cantelo.

At the second performance of *Messiah* a theatrical effect was intruded into 'Lift up your heads, O ye gates' whereby the alternating semi-chorus passages of the first section were allotted to the principal singers only, the chorus entering at bar 33. This device, we are told, 'had a most admirable effect, and brought tears into the eyes of several of the per-formers.'[3] Another novelty at the second performance was the use of trombones in 'Hallelujah' and 'Worthy is the Lamb'. And whereas on the first occasion the signal for the *encore* of 'Hallelujah' had been given (at the wish of the king) by the Earl of Sandwich, at the second performance 'his Majesty was pleased to make the signal himself, with a gentle motion of his right hand in which was the printed book of the words'.[4]

After the conclusion of the entire series of performances, there appeared a handsomely produced 'Account of the musical performances . . . in commemoration of Handel' by Charles Burney, dedicated to the king and sold for the benefit of the Musical Fund. It is from this characteristically expressed work that I have so freely quoted here in order to revive something of the contemporary flavour. Burney prefaced his account by a sketch of the life of Handel, with whom he had worked, and for whom he had coached Frasi and Guadagni. In this 'sketch' he links the Commemoration performance of *Messiah*, if not with the time of its composition, then at least with the weeks immediately following; for he recalls how, as a small boy at Chester in 1741, he saw Handel waiting to cross over to Ireland:

> I was at the Public-School in that city, and very well remember seeing him smoke a pipe, over a dish of coffee, at the Exchange-Coffee-house; for being extremely curious to see so extraordinary a man, I watched him narrowly as long as he remained in Chester; which, on account of the wind being unfavourable for his embarking at Parkgate, was several days.[5]

So Burney is able to bring our story almost full circle. Yet the Commemoration was a beginning, not an end. And, in spite of the spirit in which it was undertaken, some of us may now feel it was an unfortunate beginning. So great was its prestige that it set the pattern for monster performances in the future, performances which have utterly misrepresented Handel's style and expression. The events of 1784 mark a great divide in the history of *Messiah*, and at this point we therefore now take our leave of it.

Sources of Quotations

Chapter III

1. Townsend, Horatio, *An Account of the Visit of Handel to Dublin* . . . (Dublin, 1852), p. 50.
   Müller, Erich H., *The Letters and Writings of George Frideric Handel* (London, 1935), p. 40.
   Deutsch, Otto Erich, *Handel. A Documentary Biography* (London, 1955), p. 530
2. Townsend, p. 69; Deutsch, p. 542
3. Townsend, p. 88; Deutsch, p. 546.
4. Townsend, p. 95 forward; Deutsch, p. 550.
5. Townsend, p. 101; Deutsch, p. 553.

Chapter IV

1. Müller, p. 44; Deutsch, p. 554.
2. Deutsch, p. 563.
3. Streatfeild, R. A., *Handel* (London, 1909), p. 177; Deutsch, p. 848.
4. Deutsch, p. 588.
5. Burney, Charles, 'Sketch of the Life of Handel' prefixed to *An Account of the Musical Performances . . . in Commemoration of Handel* (London, 1785), p. 26.
6. *ibid.* p. 35.,
7. Deutsch, p. 614 forward.
8. Townsend, p. 118; Deutsch, p. 622.

Chapter V

1. Burney, Charles, *A General History of Music*, 4 vols (London, 1776-89), vol. 4, p. 449.
2. Burney, 'Sketch', p. 36.
3. Hawkins, John, *A General History of the Science and Practice of Music*, 5 vols (London, 1776), Vol. 5, p. 359.
4. *ibid.*

Chapter VI

1. Deutsch, p. 752.
2. *ibid.*, p. 813.
3. *ibid.*, p. 756 forward.
4. *ibid.*, p. 816

Chapter VII

1. Husk, W. H., *An Account of the Musical Celebrations on St Cecilia's Day* (London, 1857), p. 98.
2. *ibid.*, p. 100.
3. Deutsch, p. 804 (Wesley, *Journal*, vol. iv, p. 282).
4. Deutsch, p. 807 (Shenstone *Letters*, p. 494).

Chapter IX

1. Burney, *Account*, p. 8.
2. *ibid.*, p. 14.
3. *ibid.*, p. 112.
4. *ibid.*, p. 112.
5. Burney, 'Sketch', p. 26, footnote.

Further Reading

Dean, Winton, *Handel's Dramatic Oratorios and Masques* (London, 1959).

Larsen, Jens Peter, *Handel's Messiah: Origins—Composition—Sources* (London, 1957).

Shaw, Watkins, *A Textual and Historical Companion to Handel's 'Messiah'* (in the press).

INDEX